F.E. Field

The Green-House as a Winter Garden

A manual for the amateur

F.E. Field

The Green-House as a Winter Garden
A manual for the amateur

ISBN/EAN: 9783337256869

Printed in Europe, USA, Canada, Australia, Japan

Cover: Foto ©Lupo / pixelio.de

More available books at **www.hansebooks.com**

THE GREEN-HOUSE

AS A

WINTER GARDEN,

A

MANUAL FOR THE AMATEUR.

WITH

A LIST OF SUITABLE PLANTS AND THEIR
MODE OF CULTURE.

BY

F. E. FIELD.

WITH A PREFACE BY W. C. BRYANT.

———o———

NEW YORK:
G. P. PUTNAM & SON, 661 BROADWAY.
1869.

INDEX.

—o—

ILLUSTRATIONS.

PAGE.

Fig. 1.. 2

" 2.. 16

" 3.. 19

" 5.. 28

—o—

CONTENTS.

PAGE.

PREFACE.. 7
INTRODUCTION.. 11
GREEN-HOUSES (Aspect of).. 17
Diseases of Plants.. 35
Flower Shows.. 51
Frames and Pits.. 25
General Management of Green-houses.. 44
Green-house as a Winter Garden.. 17
Method of Heating.. 23
Potting-House.. 24
Potting.. 32
Soils and Composts.. 29
Sowing Seeds.. 42
Striking Cuttings.. 39
Summer Occupation of the Green-house.. 50
Summer Station.. 48
Watering.. 37
LIST OF PLANTS.. 53
Acacia.. 53
Azalea Indica.. 54
Cactus.. 54
Calceolaria.. 55
Camellia.. 56

PAGE.

Chorozema........ 58
Chrysanthemum........ 58
Cineraria........ 59
Correa........ 61
Coronilla........ 62
Cytisus........ 63
Daphne........ 63
Diosma........ 64
Epacris........ 64
Geranium........ 66
Heaths........ 67
Jasmin........ 68
Kennedya........ 68
Magnolia........ 69
Mignonette........ 70
Myrtle........ 71
Orange........ 71
" Otaheite........ 72
Pimelia........ 72
Polygala........ 73
Primula........ 73
Rose........ 75
Sollya........ 76
Veronica........ 76
BULBOUS ROOTED PLANTS........ 77
Amaryllis........ 77
Cyclamen........ 78
Oxalis........ 79
HYACINTHS, TULIPS, &c........ 79
Lily of the Valley........ 80
BEDDING PLANTS........ 80
ANNUALS FOR THE GREEN-HOUSE IN SUMMER........ 83
Balsams........ 83
Martynia Fragrans........ 84
Cockscomb and Amaranthus........ 84
Spomeas........ 85
Achimenes and Gloxinia........ 85

PREFACE.

The poet, Cowper, says—

"Who loves a garden, loves a green-house too."

which is certainly true so far as this, that many whose attention, if they lived in the country, would be turned to the careful cultivation of a garden, are obliged, by living in towns, to content themselves with a green-house on an humble scale, tended principally by their own care. The number of this class is increasing rapidly in our own country, and, in fact, is becoming more numerous everywhere else in the civilized world. Towns are growing larger and more compact, and the possession of a spot of cultivated land under the open sky, upon which the rains fall and the dews gather, is gradually becoming the lot of fewer and fewer of the human race. Yet, the fondness for cultivating plants, supplying them with nourishment, watching their growth, removing the causes which obstruct it, and increasing their number by skilful propagation, is a feeling so natural that it may be called instinctive. Plants minister so essentially to our comfort—they are so necessary in fact to our existence—they so gratify the love for beauty of form and color, and they show so many striking and curious adaptations, in their structure and properties, to the ends they answer, that it is not to be wondered at that their cultivation should become a passion with many.

To frame a treatise which shall instruct the increasing class to which we have referred, how to indulge this taste at a moderate expense, and by the simplest and most economical as well as most successful methods, has been the aim of the author of this little work. It is intended for those whose means or whose desires lead them to content themselves with a green-house on a small scale, to which they give their personal attention. For those who have spacious conservatories under the charge of a professional gardener, works of a more elaborate character are doubtless the best. Those, however, contain much that is only applicable to green-houses on an extensive scale, kept in order at considerable cost. They require more study and pains than many have time to bestow, and bewilder the uninitiated by the multitude and prolixity of their directions. What a person, much occupied with other pursuits, yet led by a strong inclination to that kind of culture, wants, is a set of plain and precise instructions which can be mastered without any great expense of time, and which can be easily and cheaply applied. Those who require more than this can find it in the more voluminous treatises on green-house cultivation. Those who want only this will find it here.

I was acquainted with the author of this work when he had a little green-house in England which he tended with great ingenuity and success, and without much apparent encroachment upon the time devoted to business and to reading, taking the prizes at the horticultural exhibitions of his neighborhood with a frequency which might have been a little annoying to the other members of the society by which the prizes were given. He had often thought of putting his experience in this department of horticulture into the shape of a treatise for publication. I encouraged him in this, partly for a personal reason, inasmuch as there was on my premises at Roslyn, on Long Island, a little green-house under the care of one who needed just such a plain and succinct hand-book of directions.

This is not an abridgment of any larger work; nor a compilation from other treatises, but a description of methods approved by the author's own experience, and therefore to be followed with the greater confidence of success. There are, it is true, occasional improvements made in the treatment of plants in green-houses, but the essential principles of that branch of culture remain the same, the principal changes consisting in the introduction of new plants. In this respect the caprices of fashion are often as marked as in the head dresses of women, or in other parts of the female costume. A naturalist introduces a pretty exotic from some tropical climate, and it is straightway taken into favor and becomes the reigning belle of the season. After a while, however, it takes its place among the crowd of plants from which a choice is to be made, or, perhaps, becomes altogether neglected, while the old favorites, familiar to successive generations of men, are reinstated in the place of honor which they formerly held.

It is, however, one of the advantages of the green-house that it makes us acquainted with the vegetation of countries which we are never to see, and with the structures of plants different from anything to which we are accustomed in our own climate, yet beautiful, with a strange exotic beauty, and showing how the supreme intelligence, which presided at the birth of all things, knows how to give to the grace of form a diversity without limit. I can scarcely help feeling a certain degree of pity for the man who has no inclination to become somewhat intimately acquainted with a class of existences—the individuals of the vegetable world—to which we owe so much of our comfort, and without which the world would become a bare, unpeopled desert. The green-house brings this knowledge into our dusty and crowded towns, and reproduces the aspect of the tropics in the depth of our northern winters. Every little pot of flowers which a poor woman cherishes in her humble apartment, and sets to bloom in the sunshine at her window, is the beginning of a green-house, and shows how general and spontaneous is the taste which this little work teaches to gratify in the most successful manner.

INTRODUCTION.

Of late years the increase in the number of Green-houses in England has been very great, owing partly, perhaps, to the reduced price of glass, and partly to improved and cheaper methods of construction, but mostly to an increased taste for flowers, and a desire to possess them, when our rude climate does not, unaided, afford them. At the same time it must be evident to any one having some knowledge and experience of the subject, that very many of these Green-houses present the appearance of lamentable failures.

As I have had many years' experience in the management of amateur Green-houses, and my success was grounded, first, on reading all the books I could find on the subject, then on the aid of some skilled cultivators, and lastly, on working out the results unaided, until remarkable success attended my labors, I venture to think I can give some assistance to those who seek to manage their own Green-houses; especially since, as far as I know, no manual such as is here offered, confined to the subject in hand, and yet embracing all the information necessary to the amateur cultivator, is to be found.

By Green-house, I understand, a house devoted to the culture of flowering plants which require the smallest degree of artificial heat. Let it not therefore be confounded with the cold-house, on the one hand, which requires no artificial heat, nor with the hot-house, on the other, which requires, all the year round, a temperature considerably raised; and above all, not with the vinery or fruit-house of any description.

Then the Green-house proper may be devoted to many different purposes, all of which clash more or less with each other: it is therefore, in the first place, most important to define your purpose; the want of this definite purpose being, I believe, a principal cause of the common failure spoken of: for it must ever be borne in mind, that it is impossible to cultivate successfully in the same house, plants of such different habits that some require to rest at the same time that others are in an active state.

The title I have chosen is, "the Green-house as a Winter Garden," and to such purpose alone is the present small treatise directed—to produce green leaves and flowers in the winter and spring months, when we have none in the gardens. And let it be understood that I address myself, principally, to the amateur managing his own Green-house. It will be found, I think, on experience, that a small house, so managed, affords much more pleasure and interest than much grander places, managed, however successfully, by a gardener.

The list of plants treated of is, of course, but a small portion of what it might be: I write only of what I have myself cultivated, with the results stated. It may also be remarked that those I have named are mostly of common, well known kinds, and such as are easily reared; and surely it is better to have a house full of such plants, growing and blooming in health and vigor, than the newest and choicest varieties, dwindling and with scanty bloom. At the same time let every cultivator add to the list from his own experience, never losing sight of the object in view, and taking care not to introduce plants which will not accommodate themselves to the treatment pursued.

Many shortcomings, no doubt, there are in this work ; all I hope to do is to make a step in advance of those who have preceded me.

TAUNTON, *January*, 1869.

Fig. 2. (Page 16.)

GREEN-HOUSES.

I. ASPECT.

The aspect of a Green-house, for winter culture, should be south, or a little east of it, the morning sun being more desirable than the afternoon. Circumstances may require considerable deviation from this, and much may be allowed, without preventing success, but the greatest amount of sunshine possible must be secured, and all shade of buildings or trees should as far as possible be avoided.

The form of the house will be very much determined by the situation. The simplest and cheapest is the lean-to house, as shown, Fig. 1, without side lights, and many flowers are reared successfully in such houses. Fig. 2 has front lights and a short back slope in the roof, the advantage of which is, that the inconvenience of sliding roof lights is avoided. The lights in the back slope are hung with hinges, and lifted by an iron arm and a cord attached to it passing over a pulley; a balance weight may be used with convenience. These lights may be left open without admitting rain, which can not be done by sliding lights.

If to this form of house be added a projecting frame in front, as shown in Fig. 3, a very complete house is obtained, and from my own experience I should say the most efficient working-house. The projecting frame is open to the house, excepting the necessary pillars, so that heat enough circulates in it. The plants are usually tended from the outside, the lights being hinged at top, and so easily propped up. In extreme winter weather it is possible to do the little work needed from the inside.

The span-roof house, Fig. 4, is, however, considered the most perfect form, and no doubt has many advantages, though not, I think, so many as is commonly supposed. It is no doubt the handsomer house for the display of plants, when other places are at hand in which they may be matured, but I do not think it is as good as Fig. 3 for rearing them. The upper ventilation is obtained by opening the side lights of the dormer.

It is more convenient to have the house of a

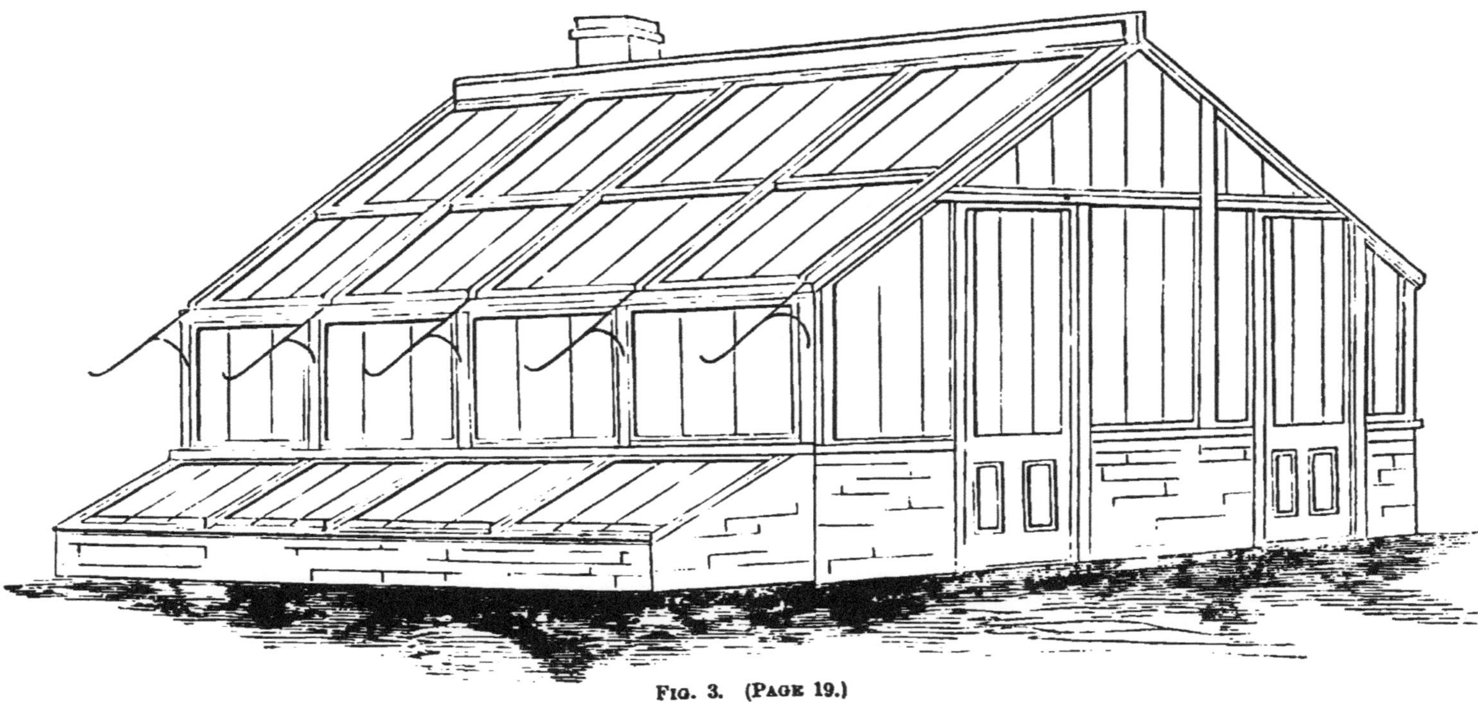

FIG. 3. (PAGE 19.)

longer and narrower form than square, as it will be found easier to arrange the plants, so that all can be reached without removing them; an inaccessible plant is apt to be neglected.

I consider it a settled question, that wooden buildings are preferable to metal; much has been written in favor of both. Beware of architectural buildings, they are generally designed with a view to appearance only, and without any regard to the purposes of the building, and however ornamental they may be, the practical working of the house is too often sacrificed.

Keep the house as low as possible, as everything thrives better near the glass. Take care that sufficient ventilation is provided; the air should circulate freely from front to back of the house, but not at the same time from end to end, and it should circulate as much as possible over the top of the plants, and not round the pots.

The glass is now put in, in such large panes that few laps are needed; when there are any, they should never be more than one-eighth of an inch, or they will cause the glass to be broken in frosty weather, from the moisture which lodges in them being frozen.

The slope of the roof should be about the angle of 45 degrees, as this slope is found to afford the greatest amount of sun-heat when it is most needed.

An outside blind, of a material known as straining canvas, is a very valuable addition; the early sunny days in spring, when the outer temperature does not admit of much ventilation, being very trying both to plants and curator. This blind should be fixed to a lath at the ridge of the house, and a roller, sufficiently heavy to keep it steadily down, attached to the other edge, running up and down the slope. There are various simple plans by which it is easily drawn up and down with a cord and a pulley. If iron arms are fixed to the roof, as shown in Fig. 3, standing out about half a yard, the front lights will be screened as well as the roof. The blind should admit of being taken down in winter.

The stages for the plants should be arranged with care; that in the centre is usually of solid brick work, and a water cistern may conveniently be within it, fed from the gutters of the roof, and with a tap for the use of the house. If this be large enough, it will usually supply water for all the house will contain.

This entire stage should be finished at the top in steps, rising about six inches, the upper one being wider than the rest, for the larger plants. The stage under the front lights should be placed the average height of a pot below the lights, so that the rain may not circulate about the pots. I prefer all these stages of solid, not open work, for the same reason, though some people do not—let them be of slate, stone or brick. Round the front and ends, a shelf about eight inches wide, and placed about six inches below the rafters, is very important; and another similar one along the back wall, pretty high up, is often useful.

II. METHOD OF HEATING.

Of the various methods of heating Green-houses, hot water circulating in large pipes is undoubtedly the best, but it is very expensive to erect in a safe and substantial manner—costing for a small house, almost as much as the buildings; nor do I consider it economical of fuel. The ordinary flue of brick, if well planned and constructed, is sufficient for common purposes, taking care to have a close fitting door, both to the ash-hole and fire-hole, with a ventilator in the former, which can be entirely closed, or opened to any extent, and so, by directing the amount of draught, the temperature of the house may be regulated to the degree required; and this, when by a little experience, the habit of the fire is understood, will be found easy. Small coal or slack well damped will always be sufficient, and by pushing the hot cinders with a long bent poker, to the back of the fire bars, and feeding it in front, it will burn with little smoke, and a fire so banked up will last, untended, for many hours.

A thermometer in the house, placed so as not to be affected by the sun's rays, is essential; and a day and night register is very desirable.

III. POTTING-HOUSE.

The amateur will find a small house or shed, where the necessary potting, &c., can be done in all weathers, very important. It should be placed, if possible, behind the Green-house, so that a door may open from the one to the other. In the plan *Fig.* 3, is shown how this may be done by extending the back slope of the roof with a slate roof, and the end of the potting-house being filled with glass uniform with the Green-house, a not unsightly arrangement results. If the fire be placed in the potting-house, with a supply of coal, the necessary attendance in bad weather is much less irksome, and there will be heat enough to keep the frost out of the potting-house, so that bulbs and other plants that are dormant in winter may be kept there.

There should be bins provided in which the various soils, &c., may be kept, so as to be available in all weathers; also shelves on which a store of pots of all sizes may be placed; and t may here be noted that all pots which have been used should be washed before they are put by, especially inside, otherwise the roots of the next plant grown in them will be very apt to adhere to the pots, rendering it impossible to turn out the ball without breaking it.

Various small utensils will be required, as potting trowels, dibbling sticks of various sizes, bell glasses, etc., and, on a substantial bench, with a good light, a large wooden potting-tray, in which the composts can be mixed and the potting done in a cleanly manner.

IV. FRAMES AND PITS.

I have now described the buildings requisite for Green-house culture; still if there can be conveniently added a common cucumber-frame, or still better a tan-pit, a more complete establishment will be formed. If both these be provided, it will be all I consider that need be desired.

The cucumber-frame is usually made square, a very inconvenient form, as the central part is difficult to reach; instead of 6 feet by 6 feet, let it be

8 feet by 5 feet. The dung hot-bed used with it is sufficient for striking cuttings and raising seeds in spring, but as the heat lasts only for a short time, it is necessary to renew it by linings of fresh manure. Later in the summer and autumn it will be useful as a cold frame.

The tan-pit, when well constructed, is a most valuable adjunct, serving much of the purpose of a forcing-house ; it should be large enough to contain at least two good cart-loads of tanner's spent bark, a less quantity does not take an effective heat. It should have brick sides and bottom, and be effectually drained, as any wet, settling in it, prevents its heating. The tan, if brought fresh from the tanner's tank, is sufficiently moist, but if it has lain some days, it will be necessary to add water before putting it into the pit. Let the pit be of such a form that all parts can be conveniently reached, and it may be from two to three feet above ground, the rest below. Some tanners use sumach, or other ingredients, the effect of which is that the tan never takes any heat, and is quite useless, but if you get proper tan and put it in in February, or early in March, it will take a good heat in a month or less, and sink down so as to afford room for the pots. This heat will last, with little variation,

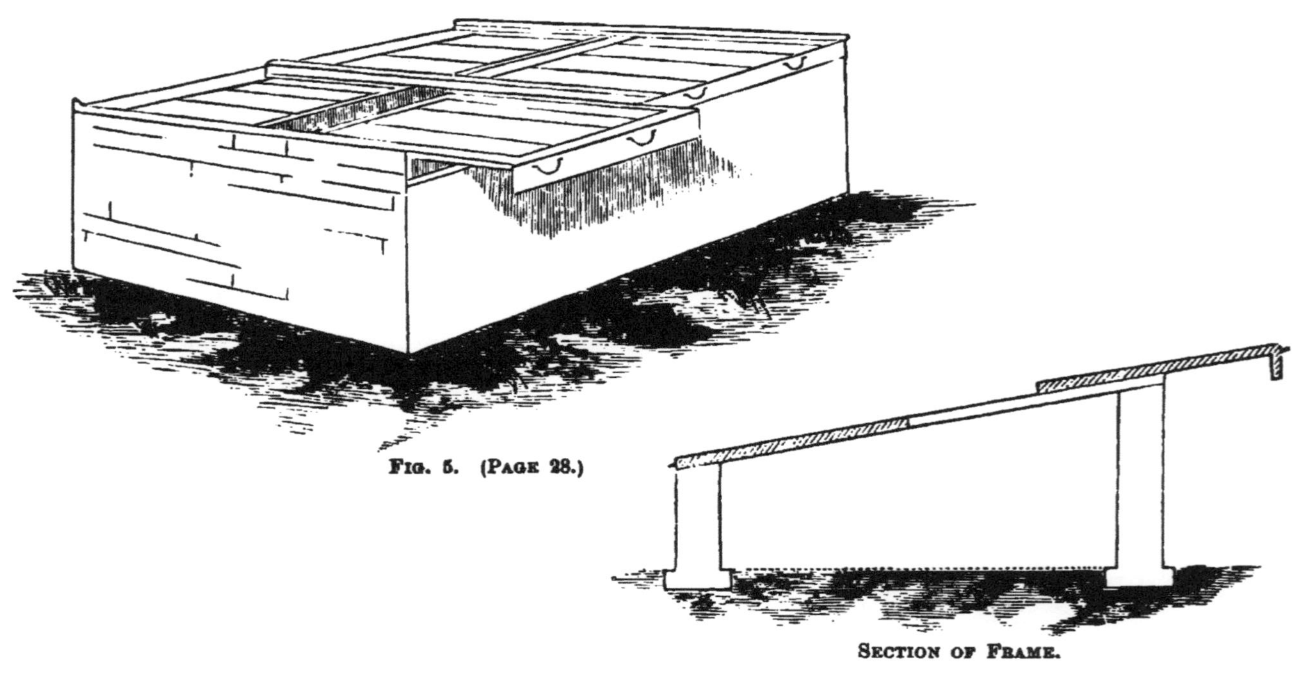

Fig. 5. (Page 28.)

Section of Frame.

throughout the summer, and even, in some degree, into the winter.

I have found great convenience in having the lights, both of the frame and tan-pit, made in half lengths, the one sliding over the other, as is shown in Fig 5. If this be done, air may be given at top and bottom at the same time, nor do the lights when open extend so inconveniently over a wide space of ground as is the case with the single light. It will be noticed that by putting a strip of wood or fillet under the upper edge of the top lights, space is obtained for the lower one to slide completely up.

The upper light is two inches wider than the lower one, and runs in a separate rabbet.

V. SOILS AND COMPOSTS.

The basis of the soil for all plants, excepting those requiring pure peat, is loam; hazel-colored loam, as the gardeners express it; this is obtained from the top-spit of good turf land; that having a mass of fibrous roots is preferred. Lay it in a heap, in the compost corner of the garden, and when the grass is dead it is fit for use, the roots remaining in the shape of fibre. This will soon be the case in the inside of the heap, though it may continue to live on the outside. Break it up in the potting tray, but do not sift it; pick out the stones and coarse, hard lumps, and look carefully for any wire-worms or other insect vermin. After a few years the root fibre decays, when a fresh heap should be prepared; therefore, it is useless to stow away too much at once.

Peat is obtained from hilly ground* where ling grows; that taken from the wet bottoms is more properly called bog, and should be avoided. Good peat is full of fibrous roots, and is of a rich purple color—bog, or exhausted peat, is black; the same change may be observed to take place in the pots. If good, it contains sufficient sand; if not, some must be added.

I have found it much better and cheaper, when the consumption is not very large, to buy it from the London nurserymen; a few bushels of Wimbledon peat will go a long way, and if kept dry in the potting-house will not materially deteriorate.

Sand should be sharp, clean, and of a light color. I have been accustomed, lately, to procure this also from the London houses. Reigate sand will save much trouble in striking cuttings, and after it has served that purpose it may be used for mixing

---

* NOTE.—As there is no ling or heath in the United States, it is suggested that leaf-mould from the woods might supply the place of the peat of Europe,—[*Editor*.

in the composts; the instructions given for the quantity to be used for the different plants is necessarily vague, since much depends upon the quality of the other ingredients. It is needed only to insure porousness of the mass, and is in itself an evil, as it occupies room and affords no nourishment.

Rotted manure, either horse or cow-dung, will be needed, but it may be thoroughly rotted down till it becomes a black friable mould.

I have sometimes obtained a very useful ingredient for composts from the tops of pollard trees, where parasitical plants have grown and left their detritus, until a rich vegetable soil has accumulated, containing abundance of the root-fibre, which, by preventing the soil in pots from caking into a hard mass, is so valuable to the floriculturist.

Some of the so-called peat which is sold at the door, cut into square pieces for burning, contains a very efficient vegetable fibre, the root being always preferable to the top. But, if nothing else is to be had, the rough fibrous part of peat must be used for the composts hereinafter directed.

Charcoal, broken to the size of hazel nuts or smaller, is used with advantage in the compost for almost all plants. It is supposed to give richness to the colors of flowers, and it is surprising how the roots will cling to it.

It is a mistake to suppose that the compost should be moist when ready for use; it is much more convenient for potting when in a dry state, but care must be taken to water sufficiently after potting.

Under the head of each plant in the list, are given instructions for mixing the suitable composts, carefully collected from the best authorities, supplemented by my own experience; but there is ample room for experiment and progress, conducted with judgment and caution. Many of the most successful cultivators differ widely in the composts they recommend for the same plant, and it should ever be borne in mind that plants in pots are in an artificial state, and it is by no means certain that their native soil is the best for them, in this artificial state.

VI. POTTING.

As all plants in pots are in an artificial state, they must be treated accordingly. Plants in the ground throw out their roots as far as they like, and seek suitable nourishment; those in pots must find it close at home, and they wind their roots round the sides of the pot, forming in a short time a ball of matted roots. It is this compression of the roots in the pot that causes plants, so cultivated, to bloom when of a smaller size, and more freely, than in their natural state, and causes also the growth of the plants to be more stinted, and their blooms smaller. The most skilful cultivator, therefore, must never hope to produce green-house plants which will bear comparison with those in their native habitat; all he can do is to try to approach it. It will be evident from this that it is not desirable to re-pot plants into larger pots too frequently; young, vigorously growing plants require such change at least once every year, sometimes even more than once; but it seems to be decided by the best authorities that old established plants, in a healthy state, may remain in the same pots for several years, not only without suffering, but with advantage, though this does not apply to all kinds of plants. The inconvenience of the large pots, with which the house is apt to get filled, has probably something to do with this opinion.

The most careful attention having been given to the mixing of the compost, the next thing is thorough drainage. Too much care cannot be taken in this matter; for if there be stagnation of wet in the pot the health of the plant is inevitably sacrificed.

After covering the hole at the bottom of the pot with a piece of broken crock, that does not lie close, so as not to prevent the water passing, throw in other smaller pieces to near an inch in depth, and over this place a layer of moss, or the coarser fibres from the vegetable soil, in such manner that the soil may not be washed down among the crocks and stop the drainage. Turn the ball out of the old pot carefully by inverting it and rapping the edge against the bench, rub away as much of the soil as you can, without damaging the roots, put as much soil in the pot as will raise the top of the ball nearly to a level with the rim, and then holding the plant upright fill round the ball. A flat strip of wood will somewhat aid this part of the process, as it is very important that no cavities be left unfilled. A rap of the bottom of the pot on the bench will shake it down, and watering settle all in its place.

The pot used in repotting should never be so much larger than the old one as to admit of more than one inch of soil round the ball, as the fresh growth of root will run immediately to the side of the pot, and the intermediate soil remain unoccupied.

Green-house plants are liable to be infested by the aphis or green fly, especially in the spring months; the only remedy I have found effective, is tobacco smoke. Take coarse waste tobacco from the manufactory, or tobacco paper used in pressing the tobacco, if it be well saturated with the juice, which much that is sold is not; break it up into pieces and damp it so that it will burn smouldering but not blazing; get an iron pot about nine inches high and six inches across, elevated a little on feet and perforated with holes in the bottom, and a larger hole at the bottom of the side where the bellows may be applied if necessary; cover the bottom with red hot cinders from the grate, shake out any dust or ashes, and throw on that a handful or two of small lumps of charcoal; then put on it the tobacco, and fill up the pot with damp moss or fine grass, plucked from the lawn; place it on the floor about the centre of the house, and start it if necessary with the bellows; if the amount of fire be proportioned to the dampness of the tobacco, it will burn out slowly without blazing till all is gone.

An evening free from much wind should be chosen, and if it be raining all the better, as the rain will close the openings of the laps in the glass. Every aperture should be carefully shut, and if it is thoroughly done the house will look as white as an egg from the outside, and you will not be able to see across it. It should not be opened again till morning.

It is well to repeat the operation two evenings in succession, using a smaller dose the second time; this will destroy those insects which were able to survive the first application.

Some recommend the use of saltpetre in damping the tobacco, and this no doubt causes it to burn more freely, but I do not consider it necessary, if a reasonable degree of pains be taken, and there can be no doubt that the effluvia given off by saltpetre is more or less injurious to all plants.

Mildew attacks some plants; it is easily cured by dusting fine powdered sulphur over and under the leaves and on the stems, either with a fine dredger, or better, by flinging it from a camel-hair brush—a repetition of it may be necessary.

Worms in the pots, though not a disease, may come under this head. They do much mischief by appropriating the vegetable matter of the soil, and leaving in their casts a very adhesive refuse, which soon converts the soil in the pot to a sodden mass, so that all proper drainage is prevented.

Their presence will be discovered by worm casts on the surface, and on turning out the ball they may usually be found next the side of the pot, and so be readily removed. Sometimes they will come to the surface on tapping the side of the pot; but if these methods fail, use the clear water of quick-lime.

VIII. WATERING.

Rain-water is the best for all plants, and if that from the roof be carefully saved within the house, it is all that can be desired, as it will generally be of the same temperature as the house; plants are often injured by being watered with cold water. If rain should fall soon after the roof has been painted and before the paint is dry, it will poison the water so as to be injurious to the plants, and the use of it must then be avoided.

I need not further enlarge upon the necessity of careful drainage, after what has been said under the head of potting; on its success more than on anything, depends the health and life of the plants; and if that be neglected, watering becomes a great difficulty, but if that be attended to, it is perfectly easy. You must never be content with any general watering of the plants; but examine each one separately, and water none but such as require it, and, when you do water, give enough to wet the ball all through and the surplus will run off through the drainage. The ladies' plan of giving a little water every day is most fatal to plants, the result being that the surface is kept moist, while the active roots which are below get no water, and the plant dwindles and dies.

It will be asked when does a plant require water? I answer, when the ball is dry, and it should on no account be left dry till the plant droops. Experience alone will entirely master this difficulty, if the directions given above be followed. It is certain that if the surface of the soil is moist, no water is required; if it be dry, a tap on the side of the pot with the knuckle will generally be answered by a solid or hollow sound, indicating that the ball is moist or dry; sometimes the weight of the-pot to one accustomed to their management, is a sufficient guide, and the same experience will soon establish a general knowledge of the individual wants of the plants, according to the weather, to their more or less active state, and the amount of firing which has been used.

After all, it may not unfrequently be necessary to turn the plant out of the pot to ascertain its condition, an error either way being much to be deprecated, especially in winter culture. If a plant be continually moist when, being in an active state, it might be supposed to want water, it will be most commonly found that, owing to worms, or some other cause, the drainage is imperfect.

Plants in peat, or even in a large proportion of fibrous vegetable soil, will, if they have become thoroughly dry, at first reject the water like a dry sponge; this state is indicated by the water running through almost as soon as it is given at top, none in fact being absorbed; in such case either plunge the pot in a bucket of water or let it stand with a pan full of water under it twenty-four hours.

I believe this little difficulty to be the reason why it is commonly thought that Heaths, Epacris and such plants, are difficult to cultivate, but this being mastered, I consider no class of plants more desirable for the amateur's winter house, especially as they are entirely free from the aphis and other Green-house diseases.

IX. STRIKING CUTTINGS.

As a general rule, cuttings strike more freely if taken from the lower part of the plants near the roots. Let them be of the last growth, with an eye at the base, and never very long. I should almost say the shorter the better. Some cultivators say this eye is better of the growth of the previous year, the rest of the cutting being of new wood. I believe it is so in some kinds of plants, not in all. Let the amateur experiment for himself; cut off the cutting clean at the base, with a sharp knife, not scissors, it being most important not to bruise the cutting; all leaves on the lower part should likewise be removed carefully with a sharp knife, taking care not to injure the bark.

The surest plan with all cuttings, is to plant them in clean sand, laid about one inch thick over the soil suitable to the plants in hand: use a wide-mouthed pot or seed-pan, and having prepared the cuttings as directed, moisten the sand so as to give it sufficient consistency; take a dibble with the end cut off square, and make the holes for the cuttings as near as possible to the depth of the sand, but not through it; place the cutting in the hole and press the sand round it till it stands firmly in its place, bearing in mind that the important point is, that the base of the cutting rest firmly on sand. If a pointed dibble is used, there is inevitably a cavity between the base of the cutting and the sand, which is sure to interfere with success.

When the pan is filled with cuttings, water carefully with a fine syringe, to settle the sand firmly down; a bell glass should then cover the whole; no cutting should touch another or the side of the glass. Bottom-heat will aid the striking of all cuttings if a hot-bed or tan-pit be available, though many of the hardier kinds will succeed without.

Bell-glasses should not be so flat at top as to allow the drops condensing from evaporation to fall upon the cuttings; they should run down the sides, and the glasses be taken off every day and wiped dry inside, any excess of moisture being injurious.

The object of this arrangement will be readily understood; it is that the cuttings should have sufficient moisture about them to sustain life until they make their own roots, and so provide their own nourishment, the sand allowing all surplus moisture, which would tend to decay, to pass off, and the soil necessary for their support being within reach as soon as they can make use of it.

The cutting-pans should be carefully shaded from the sun, and as even a temperature as possible secured; they will occasionally require watering with a fine syringe, as will be known by the sand feeling loose to the finger, and not consistent; after watering leave the glass off for a short time, so that what falls on the tops of the cuttings may dry up, but avoid exposing them long enough to droop.

When the cuttings have taken root they will begin to grow, and should then be potted into thumb pots, and replaced in the temperature they were struck in, and then gradually hardened to their natural exposure.

In striking cuttings without bell-glasses or bottom-heat, of such plants as geraniums, chrysanthemums, &c., place the cuttings close to the sides of the pot, in a compost of one-half their proper soil and one-half sand, press the soil firmly to the cuttings, water slightly, and place them in the shade; they will not strike so surely, or so soon, as under the treatment previously directed, but it may sometimes be more convenient to adopt this plan.

X. SOWING SEEDS.

As a general rule, seeds which ripen before midsummer should be sown immediately, as there is then time enough to produce plants to bloom the next winter or early spring season; seeds ripened or obtained later than that, had better be reserved till the following spring. There are exceptions, which will be noticed under the head of individual plants.

New seed is preferable in almost all cases—there are some exceptions, however, to this rule also, in the case of semi-double flowered plants, which will be mentioned in the proper place.

It is a great fault to sow seeds too deeply—the slightest possible covering is sufficient for small seeds, increasing it as they increase in size. In some cases it is even desirable not to cover the seeds at all, but sow them on the surface and lay a flat piece of glass over the rim of the pot, taking off the glass when the seeds begin to grow.

The soil should always be firm and light, and for a covering firm sand is successfully used. Water slightly, with a fine syringe, after sowing, and from time to time as may be needful to keep the soil damp but never wet. As soon as they begin to grow place them near the glass that they may not be drawn to dwindling plants; they will require very careful watching in all their stages. As soon as they show their second leaves, or can be handled, prick them off each an inch or so apart, mostly close to the sides of the pot, and if available, give them bottom heat for a week or ten days. As soon as the plants touch one another pot them singly into thumb pots, repeating the bottom heat, and when the roots are matted to the sides of the pots, re-pot them into larger pots, and harden them gradually to their natural temperature.

In all the early stages of seedling plants, shading from the sun heat, if powerful, must be provided; a piece of paper over the pots is a convenient plan, taking care that it does not touch the plants.

XI. GENERAL MANAGEMENT OF THE GREEN-HOUSE.

Early in September the season of the winter garden may be said to commence; later than that it is not desirable to leave the plants out of doors. Let the house be well cleaned, the walls whitewashed, and it is my custom to give the wood-work inside a coat of paint every year. Clean out the water-cistern, that there may be no foul smell; see that the heating apparatus is in working order, and everything so cared for that no repairs be needed in the winter.

Let the pots be well cleaned, the balls turned out, to ascertain that all are in a healthy state, and all dead wood or leaves be removed. The surface soil should be scraped off as far as can be done without injuring the roots, and a top dressing of the proper compost supplied. Any weak herbaceous plants or straggling branches should be tied up, that all may look neat, and every plant stand over its own pot.

Look well that no hidden snail or other vermin get into the house, and if the green fly be on any of the plants, apply tobacco smoke as directed.

The plants must not be crowded together—a free circulation of air around each is indispensable. Cleanliness is highly important, so that no impure air arise from dirty places, damp leaves, or decaying flowers.

All surplus water running from the pots should be taken up with a sponge, as well as that from condensation on the glass. No dwelling room needs to be sweeter than the Green-house if it be desired to see the plants thrive.

In placing the plants upon the stages, judgment must be used, to give as far as possible an equal share of light to each, rather more to the feebler than the stronger plants; and although the taller ones will naturally be placed at the back of the centre stage, and shorter ones in front, do not for the sake of appearance put feeble plants behind. All should be within reach, and should be turned round from time to time, that all sides may have the benefit of the indispensable light.

Herbaceous plants must be placed as near the glass as possible, till they are in flower, as otherwise the stems will grow weak. The projecting frame (Fig. 3) is the best place for them.

If the directions given have been attended to in their proper season, spring will now be commencing in the Green-house, as winter begins in the garden; and to the manager of his own Green-house it is, I think, the most interesting time of the year—the replacing of the loss of the natural summer by an artificial one—although it be but a humble imitation; and the object, in the management of the house, should be to encourage bloom by placing the plants in circumstances similar to summer, the season of natural bloom, and therefore though artificial heat is always an evil, it is under these circumstances a necessary evil.

When the plants are first housed after passing all the summer out of doors, they will show a tendency to droop, and as much ventilation day and night must be given as can safely be done; but cross-currents of air must be avoided, and if the front and roof lights are slightly opened, the doors must be closed.

If the weather be sunny, as it often is, no fire will be required, the sun-heat being sure to raise the temperature sufficiently in the day, and any slight frost which may occur at night will be guarded against by early closing; but a succession of damp, gloomy days must be counteracted by a little fire in the day time, with the lights open, taking care that the fire is out and the flue cooled down by the time it becomes necessary to close the house; too high a temperature at night is injurious.

As the winter advances, let the temperature maintained be not under 40 at night, nor over 50 or 55 in the day, and though it may raise higher by sun-heat, it should never rise higher by artificial heat, always bearing in mind that air must be admitted on every favorable occasion.

Chrysanthemums will be first in bloom, and though they are better grown out of doors, where climate and situation permit, yet a few small plants grown as directed will be valuable in the house, since they fill an interval of bloom, as no other plant will. They may stand on the floor or other places, even if they cause a little crowding for a short time, and be removed to the cold frame when their bloom is over, requiring but little attention till the spring.

Next will follow Primula, Cineraria, Epacris, Cytisus, Azalea, Camellia, and other plants named in the following list, keeping up a succession of bloom until the garden flowers resume their beauty in June. The Geranium I consider the last of the list.

These directions need little variation throughout the winter. As spring advances air should be given more abundantly, to prepare the plants for full exposure out of doors in the summer months, leaving the lights open at night, when it can be safely done.

Early in June the weather generally admits of the whole being removed to their summer station; some hardier ones may have been put out earlier. The general repotting of the plants at this time, which forms so important a feature in the directions given in many books, will be superseded by the progressive attention given to them, as directed under the head of each kind of plant.

XII. SUMMER STATION.

The choice of the summer station, where the plants may have full exposure during the months of June, July and August, is a very important matter; on it success will very much depend; scarcely any winter-blooming Green-house plant will thrive without it. I lay down what I consider the conditions to be aimed at; let them be approached as nearly as circumstances will admit. It should be exposed to about half the day's sunshine, the morning part being preferable; well sheltered from boisterous winds, which blow the plants down or break them; there should be room enough for the plants to stand well apart, that the air may circulate freely around them; every pot should stand level, so that it may be freely watered without its running over, and upon a floor of asphaltum, brick, stone, or fine coal ashes and lime, well beaten down, otherwise worms will get into the pots, and the roots will run out at the bottom and take hold of the ground, thus causing a severe check to the plants when they are moved.

In default of a permanent arrangement for the floor of the summer station, tiles or slates may be laid down and propped to a level surface.

Some careful cultivators prop slates or tile against the sides of the pots to protect them from the heat of the sun, it being an evil to the roots, though a great benefit to the tops.

Careful watching will be needed, that the plants do not suffer from want of water, as, being in an active and growing state, much will be required; frequently more than one soaking a day will be needed, and even in rainy weather a bushy plant will get but little water to the soil. If any get too much soaked with rain they may be laid down on their sides for twenty-four hours or more without serious injury. It may be desirable to tie up tall plants to sticks, stuck in the ground, to prevent their being blown over. In warm evenings syringe them well overhead or use a watering pot with a fine rose. Some prunings of rampant growth may occasionally be necessary, and dead leaves and insects must be removed.

XIII. SUMMER OCCUPATION OF THE GREEN-HOUSE.

When the proper occupants of the Green-house are removed to their summer station, the house may be filled with annuals, of which Balsams will form the principal and a very beautiful feature. If good seeds be procured, and they are grown as directed into fine branching plants, twenty or thirty of them will fill a small Green-house with a splendor not easily surpassed. Some of the hot-house Ipomeas (I. cerulea, &c.) may be added, running up strings fastened in festoons to the roof, also cockscomb, amaranthus, &c.

If the tan-pit be in operation, much more may be done, as many hot-house plants which are dormant in winter may be cultivated, the Green-house being used as a hot-house in summer, and this class of plants started in the tan-pit. Of these, Gloxinias, one of the most beautiful exotics we have, is perfectly available, and may be grown in great perfection. Achimenes, Martynia, and many others may be added.

The house, as before said, must now be treated as a hot-house. The plants will require an abundance of water and almost constant shading in the day. It must be closed early to secure a temperature through the night proportioned to that in the day, firing not being, in this case, needed. Syringe overhead, as much as possible without injuring the bloom, when the house is closed at night, and water the stages and floor. If the house have the full morning sun, the curator must be stirring early, or the temperature will be raised to too high a point before the air is given.

XIV. FLOWER SHOWS.

Let the amateur beware of being tempted to grow plants for exhibition at flower-shows. When great success has been attained it is a temptation to display that success; but it will be found to involve a terrible sacrifice. Professed growers usually giving their attention to a few kinds of plants, and having various costly appliances to enable them to attain excellence, become the opponents of the amateur with his small establishment, and it will be found necessary to sacrifice the bulk of the collection for the sake of a few favored specimens, and the honor of taking a few prizes will be a very inadequate recompense.

A little experience will satisfy the amateur that it is not an easy thing to prepare and keep plants so as to be fit for exhibition on a certain day; then the plants for the sake of which all the others have suffered, become themselves much injured by the carriage and exposure; and the result is a depreciation of the whole collection which a year will scarcely restore.

Until managers of exhibitions contrive to classify the specimens with some reference to the means of exhibitors, and this is not easy, flower-shows must be avoided by the amateur who manages his own Green-house.

A LIST OF PLANTS

Suitable for the Green-house as a Winter Garden, with their soils and mode of culture, and the names of some desirable varieties.

Acacia.

Armata. Cunninghami. Prostrata.

Soil, two parts loam, one vegetable fibre, one sand.

There is not much variety in the flower, though there is in the foliage, one or two plants are deisrable; they are very easily cultivated, but not easy to be grown into handsome pyramidal plants; their growth is apt to be wild and straggling, but they bloom freely and early in the year. As soon as they begin to grow after bloom is over, cut back the long shoots, leaving two or three eyes of the last growth, and having regard to the form of the plant; the pyramidal being always aimed at, shorten the leader well back. When a decided growth is starting after pruning, repot, but avoid increasing the size of the pot as much as possible, or the plants will soon get too large for the house. They grow very rapidly, and it is desirable to get them out of the warm Green-house as soon as possible, lest they make weak wood.

Azalea Indica.

Gledstanesii. *Danielsiana.* *Variegata.* *Alba Lutescens,* and the *Old Alba* for its delicious scent.

Soil, two parts peat, one loam and sand, one rotted manure.

One of the most beautiful plants we have, and with ordinary care it grows into fine specimens. Some growers use a stronger soil than I have given, and if larger and wilder growing plants are desirable, they are right, but for a small establishment it is better rather to check than encourage the size of the plants. They, in common with all plants that grow in a large proportion of peat, require much water as the flower buds swell and while blooming. The new growth shows itself often before the bloom is over. They do not require much pruning, just enough to keep the plant shapely. Repot as soon as the bloom is over, if the new growth be started; and keep them in the warm house till the general clearing out, in June.

CACTUS.

Speciosissimus. *Ackermannii.* *Crenatus.*

Soil, three parts sandy loam, one part charcoal, and pot-sherds broken to the size of hazel nuts.

A beautiful plant in bloom; very unsightly when not in bloom. It is almost dormant in the autumn and early winter months, and should be kept cool and almost without water till it shows signs of growth. When started the growth is rapid and requires abundant watering till the bloom is over, and it must be freely encouraged till the next growth is made. I do not consider many of them desirable, but they are easily managed. No pruning is necessary.

In their dormant state the shelf in the potting house is the best place.

CALCEOLARIA.

Soil, two parts loam, one part rotted manure, and one of coarse vegetable fibre or peat and sand—a very open compost being desirable.

This plant, owing to the hybrid culture it has received, has become nearly an annual; that is to say it is almost necessary to raise them every year from seeds; cuttings may be struck from very successful varieties, but, according to my experience, with difficulty and doubtful result.

Seed should be sown as soon as it is ripe, and on the surface of the seed-pan, not covered at all, but with a flat plate of glass laid over the rim of the pan and the pan placed in a warm part of the house near the glass or in the pit of the pan. As soon as it is up, fine sand should be sprinkled over it and a bell-glass substituted for the flat plate. In all its stages just enough water must be given to promote growth, but not enough to cause the plants to damp off, and as soon as possible give some air daily.

The plants should be fit to pot into thumb-pots, and get established in them before winter, giving them a little close treatment after the change, and in these pots they had better remain till early in the spring, when a disposition to active growth will appear, and they may be potted into blooming-pots about four and a half inch; after this keep them as near the glass as possible, water in proportion to the capacity of their state, and guard against the aphis by tobacco smoke.

CAMELLIA.

Double White and Red. Lady Hume. Celestina. Eclipse.

Soil—One part loam, one part sand, one part vegetable fibre, and one part rotted manure.

Very various are the instructions of different writers for the treatment of this plant, as regards the compost and all other points of management. All agree that it is very hardy and easily managed. I must candidly confess that it is the only plant with which I have not attained satisfactory success. The compost I have directed appears to me the most hopeful. It readily makes its growth under the treatment directed for the winter garden, and readily sets its buds, but when it ought to bloom, the buds are apt to fall off.

It is perhaps the most beautiful winter-blooming plant we have, and is worthy the utmost care to insure success, but it must take its chance with its companions in a mixed Green-house. No doubt it is very important to have healthy plants to begin with, and this is easily ascertained by turning them out of the pot before they are purchased; if there be not healthy roots outside the ball reject them. Water them according to their state of activity; freely when growing or opening their blooms, otherwise sparingly, but do not let them get dry so as to droop. They must be repotted soon after they begin to grow and the bloom is over, and any straggling branches shortened; but usually little pruning is needed.

CHOROZEMA.

Varia. Ilicifolia. Rhombea. Nana.

Soil—Two parts peat, one part loam, taking care there is sufficient sand.

A very pleasing, half-climbing plant; some of them may be grown as shrubbery plants, but they are more usually trained to a trellis. If it be attempted to grow them without training, the growth, which will start freely after blooming, must be checked by stopping the ends of the shoots. Repot them when the new growth is fairly started. In common with all plants whose compost consists largely of peat, they require much attention in watering. If they be allowed to get quite dry, and it be not perceived, when they are watered, that the water all runs through, a day or two will kill the plant.

CHRYSANTHEMUM.

The varieties are endless. The pompons are perhaps the most eligible for the Green-house, as they make more bushy plants, and the flowers are very valuable for bouquets.

Soil—three parts loam, one part sand.

Small plants for the Green-house may be raised by taking the ends of the long shoots in June or

July, and placing them in sand under glass, if convenient, if not, put them round the sides of the pot and in a shady place. If a number of plants be required for any festive decoration, layer the ends of the long shoots in pots, plunged around the parent plant.

When rooted, pot them singly into small pots, and as soon as they will bear it, bring them to the light. One other shift into five-inch pots will be sufficient and they will be ready to go into the house with the other plants in September. As soon as the bloom is over, cut them back, and put them in the cold frame, or plunge them in a sheltered place. They must be attended to in the spring, so as to encourage the growth in time for next year's cuttings, which is best done by planting them out in the ground, and if they are wanted for the borders they may be put there and the cuttings taken at the time directed.

By taking the cuttings from the ends of the long shoots, more bushy plants are produced than f the shorter shoots are taken from the lower part of the plants.

CINERARIA.

Soil, two parts loam, one part vegetable fibre, one part rotted manure, and sand added.

One of the most valuable plants for Winte rdecoration ; easy of culture, sure of success and with an almost endless variety of bloom, Like the Calceolaria, it is now most usual to grow them every year from seed. Gather the seed as it ripens, choosing the best flowers, and sow it very slightly covered as soon as you get it—though, if a hot bed or tan-pit be in preparation, wait for that—if kept just moist and shaded it soon comes up; and the plants, as soon as they can be handled, may either be pricked off into seed-pans, or large pots, two inches apart each way, or put at once singly into thumb-pots; shade them till they start, giving a little heat if available. Through the summer they should be grown in a cold frame, the pots plunged in sand or ashes. Shift them twice, finally into five-inch pots.

Be watchful for the Aphis, to which the plant is peculiarly liable. Tobacco smoke must be applied, but in a frame it requires care not to scorch the plants. Shade them from the mid-day sun, and shut the frame close or nearly so at night. I consider it desirable to rub off from time to time all the shoots but the centre one with a blunt pointed stick, and of course it must be done with care, as a much handsomer plant is the result, and much earlier bloom. If it be desired to propagate any variety, it is easily done by taking the young shoots from the roots, which make their appearance soon after the old blooming stem is cut away, and often earlier. If their off-shoots be not rooted, as they generally are, they must be struck in cuttings; if rooted, put them into thumb-pots. In either case give them a little heat, or close treatment, and keep them as above directed with the seedlings, in the cold frame through the summer.

If this culture be successfully carried out, there may be any desired number of these beautiful plants, in health and luxuriance, ready to take their place in the winter garden. They will begin to bloom by Christmas, or even before, and continue till May or June.

As soon as the bloom of any plant is over, cut it back, if it be wished to save cuttings, and put it in any corner among the other pots, but not too much shaded. Water but sparingly till fresh growth starts from the roots. Any not desired for propagation may be at once thrown away; they are useless for the borders.

CORREA.

Alba. Pulchella. Speciosia. Rosea.

Soil—Two parts peat, one part loam, one sand.

This plant requires a treatment similar to the Chorozema. It is not one of the most eligible, but it forms a pleasing variety in a winter-blooming collection. Stop the free growing shoots, to promote a bushy habit, and do not repot too freely. It will bear in all respects the general treatment directed.

CORONILLA.

Glauca. Valentina.

Soil—Two parts loam, one vegetable fibre, one sand.

A pretty yellow flower, rather too free a grower; it blooms early in the year and is useful for the winter garden, though not one of the most eligible. It bears very free pruning after the bloom is over, and indeed requires it, the growth being inclined to be straggling; two eyes in the last growth are enough to leave, and in some cases it may even be cut back into that of the previous year. Repot as soon as the new growth is started, but avoid increasing the size of the pots more than is necessary. With vigorous plants the ball may be reduced by picking away the old soil with a pointed stick, and even cutting off some of the longer roots. It will bear putting out of doors early.

CYTISUS.

Racemosa. Rhododpahne.

Soil—Two parts loam, one vegetable fibre, one sand.

Like the last subject, a wild grower, and requires similar treatment. Flowers yellow, with all the sweetness of the wild broom and very abundant. It is valuable as a free winter-blooming plant.

DAPHNE.

Indica. Odora.

Soil—Two parts loam, one part peat, taking care there is sufficient sand. Some growers add a little rotted manure; but I doubt the wisdom of this.

No flower can be more valuable; if the plant can be kept in a reasonably symmetrical form, it is beautiful and has an exquisite scent; it is, however, very difficult to do so. With old plants grown to long, bare stems, it is hopeless to do anything; but if young ones be carefully treated, they may be tolerated for a few years. Sometimes it will answer to cut them back within a few inches of the crown of the root; but sometimes they will not break again. It is always safe to cut them back to an eye or two of the last growth, and if not too much stimulated, they will break freely from those eyes. Too rapid a growth is the thing to be feared, for that causes the long bare stems. Get them out of doors or in a cold frame as soon as possible, and keep them out as long as can safely be done. But with all possible care it will probably be necessary to tie them to props, and even then they will very likely be soon discarded. Of course, no pruning must be done till after the bloom is over, as it always comes at the ends of the shoots.

DIOSMA.

Umbellata. Fragrans. Ericoides.

Soil—three parts peat, one part loam.

A very charming evergreen heath-like shrub, with an aromatic, and to some people, most agreeable scent from the foliage; very valuable as green for a bouquet, though of late much neglected. It grows luxuriantly into a fine bushy plant, and continues flowering throughout the early spring, though the flowers are insignificant. It may be pruned almost at will into any form, after blooming, and must not be over-potted.

EPACRIS.

Wilmareana. Variabilis. Impressa. Miniata. Grandiflora. Campanulata rubra.

Soil—peat, with sufficient sand.

Some growers recommend a small addition of loam, but I doubt the propriety of this.

One of the most valuable of the winter-blooming plants, sometimes called the Australian heath, and in most respects similar to the heath. The tubular-shaped flowers are of considerable variety, and make a very elegant admixture with others, either in the house or in a bouquet, If it has made a free growth after the previous bloom, and the wood is matured, a fine bloom is safe for the succeeding season. It requires abundant watering when coming to bloom, and plenty of light, and starts its growth freely afterwards, but sometimes needs a little close treatment in the cold frame to encourage luxuriance. Cut back freely after the bloom is over, but never beyond the wood or the last growth; re-pot as soon as it breaks, and put them into the cold frame as soon as is safe; that is a little before the other plants go to the summer station; they are better plunged in sand or ashes. Close the lights early in the evening, and shade from the hot mid-day sun, in a few weeks more then to the summer station.

Grandiflora, Miniata, and some others of similar habits, are difficult to grow without training to a trellis, but most of them will, with care, make bushy plants.

GERANIUM.

Varieties endless. Soil—two parts loam, one part rotted manure, one part vegetable fibre, one part sand.

The beauty and value of this plant, with its immense variety, is known to every one; nothing is more easily cultivated, but more convenient plants for a small collection may be produced by careful attention, than are usually grown. It is desirable to have young plants every two, or at least, every three years, and they strike so easily from cuttings that this may be done with little labor. They require but a very reasonable share of attention in the house, and are almost the latest bloomers in the winter collection. Put them back freely when the bloom is over, and as the time for moving the collection out of doors will be at hand, do not wait for the few last straggling flowers; they may even be cut into the old wood partially, and the tops used for striking plants for the borders, or new plants for the collection. They will strike freely under the bell-glass in sand, or without, but in the latter case of course not so soon. Young plants will not be fit to take their place in the collection the first season, but may be kept in small pots and placed among the others out of the way. The next spring they should be cut back to within a few eyes of the soil, re-potted as soon as they start, and subjected to the general treatment. The second season they will replace the old ones, which may be discarded. The Geranium loves free pot-room, and on this plan you can afford to give it. If old plants be kept longer than I have indicated, the balls may be pared down to keep them in more convenient sized pots, but they will never be so satisfactory as young plants.

HEATHS.

Hyemalis, Gracilis, Flammea, Wilmereana and others.

Soil—Peat and sand.

Be watchful that the drainage is efficient, never neglect watering when the plant requires it, and give as much air as possible, do not crowd them with other plants. Half a dozen Heaths, judiciously selected can hardly be dispensed with, in the smallest collection. If they be not crowded or watering neglected, both of which faults cause base or "*rusty*" stems, they will grow and improve for many years. Young plants require re-potting every year, but old ones have been known to do well in the same pot for three or four years, not of course making much growth; but that is not needed. Unless the growth be unusually rampant, little pruning is required beyond cutting back such shoots as interfere with a good form of plants, and this may always be safely done if you keep within the last growth. The heath is so elegant a plant that it is worth a little extra trouble if indeed it requires it; and if the directions, given under the head "Watering," be attended to, I do not think it will be found more troublesome than other plants.

Re-pot, if needed, when the fresh growth has started, and put the plants out of doors, as early as is safe.

JASMINE.

Grandiflorum. Hirsutum.

Soil—one part loam, one part vegetable fibre, one part rotted manure.

Except for their exquisite fragrance, these are not desirable plants; their growth is awkward and uncontrollable; they require no unusual care; prune them freely and do not stimulate the growth.

KENNEDYA.

Inophylla. Monophylla. Eximia.

Soil—three parts peat, one part loam and sand.

A very charming climbing plant; must be trained; a most abundant bloomer, and in every respect very desirable. It makes luxuriant growth, and must be pruned accordingly, when the bloom is over. The difficulty is to keep it within compass, either in the top or roots. Young plants may be readily raised, either from cuttings or layers. It requires abundant watering when in bloom, for, if in good health, it bears very numerous trusses of flowers, and is as beautiful as any plant in the winter collection. It must not be put out of the house till it has started its fresh growth.

MAGNOLIA.

The Chinese species and their hybrids, *Fuscata, Soulangiana, Conspicua.*

Soil—two parts peat, one part loam and sand.

Treatment the same as the Camellia. I have not had much success with this plant, and do not strongly recommend it. Soulangiana when well grown and bloomed is fine; but I have found it difficult to treat in both respects. It does not bear any comparison with the American species, either in size of flower or richness of foliage. The more out-door treatment it gets the better.

MIGNONETTE.

Soil—two parts loam, one part rotted manure, one part sand.

For winter bloom, a few plants are desirable; but though it is easy to grow them with a few stunted flowers, it is not easy to grow them well.

If it be desired to rear it as a single plant, trained in the form of a tree, the seeds should be sown in June, in thumb-pots, three or four seeds in each, and when they are fairly up remove all but one; re-pot this, from time to time, up to the size of about a five-inch pot, keeping it in a shady place, and pinching off the blooms as soon as they appear; if the growth is not luxuriant enough, use liquid manure or guano; water once a week, and at all times avoid over watering—indeed, in heavy rains, the plants should be sheltered. In this manner fine large plants may be grown, and as soon as the Green-house plants are housed they may be allowed to bloom, and will continue to do so all through the winter.

If you are content with smaller plants and less trouble, sow the seed in August, in the pots it is intended they should bloom in, and when up, thin out to three or four plants, and treat them in the same manner as above directed. This plant always succeeds best if transplanting be avoided.

MYRTLE.

Single. Double. Narrow-leaved. Broad-leaved.

Soil—One-half loam, one-half vegetable fibre and sand.

Though not properly a winter flowering plant, yet it will gradually accommodate itself to the temperature of the house, and blossom early in spring, and surely no more beautiful plant can be grown; its habit is good and its foliage charming. It requires very little pruning; what is cut for bouquets, if judiciously done, will probably be enough. The difficulty is to avoid getting them into pots so large as to be inconvenient; avoid, therefore, increasing the size as much as possible, and though young plants will require repotting every year, older ones may be kept two years in the same pot, even if the growth become somewhat stunted. It is nearly hardy, and may be put out of doors early, and if disposed to blossom after this, pinch off the blossom buds.

ORANGE.

Soil—Two parts loam, one part rotted manure, one part vegetable fibre—sand if neéded.

A fine evergreen plant, not easy to rear in good form and habit; but with some trouble, the scent of the flower, as every one knows, is exquisite, and the fruit forms a handsome feature in a winter group. It requires perfect drainage, abundant water when in active growth, and occasionally liquid manure, and syringing overhead. Pruning must be done with judgment, as by cutting away the young growth you lose the blossom of next season; still this must be done to some extent, if the plant makes one-sided and awkward growth. It must be repotted if full of roots, and if the ball feel dry and hard, soak it first. Unfortunately the results of successful treatment will probably be, that the plant will get too large for the house.

ORANGE, OTAHEITE.

A dwarf species, rather recently introduced; it is compact in habit and does not grow more than eighteen inches in height; it is not so handsome in foliage as the common orange, but has the same sweet scent, and is more manageable as a Green-house plant, and very desirable. It requires the same treatment.

PIMELIA.

Intermedia. Linifolia. Rosea. Spectabilis.

Soil—Three parts peat, one part loam, sand and charcoal.

A very pleasing evergreen shrub; requires a

treatment similar to the Epacris, careful drainage, and watering. It must be cut back after blooming, but not beyond the wood of the last growth, and repotted as soon as a fresh growth is started, and unless it be very luxuriant it should have the shelter of the cold frame for a few weeks before it is removed to the summer station.

POLYGALA.

Oppositifolia. Grandiflora. Gracilis.

Soil—three parts peat, one part loam and sand.

A pretty pea-shaped flower, but rather a wild grower, in other respects easily managed; it is a free bloomer, and comes early in the year. Cut back freely into the last growth, and even into the older wood partially; use as few props as possible, but some will be needed, as the shoots are apt to be weak; abundance of air is the best corrective, but it will not bear to be exposed out of doors too early.

PRIMULA.

Sinensis, single and double, pink and white. Cortusoides. Nivalis. Verticillata. Farinosa, &c.

Soil—two parts vegetable fibre, using the rougher part with charcoal and sand; a very open compost being desirable.

The fringed varieties of the pink and white single *sinensis*, are most eligible plants for winter culture. Sow the seed early in June, on a slight heat, if available ; if not, in a warm corner of the Green-house, covered with a flat piece of glass. Prick out the plants singly in thumb-pots, as soon as they can be handled, and give them a little close treatment, till they are rooted ; after that keep them in the cold frame with the cinerarias, &c., potting them up into five-inch pots as they need it. They are free growing, beautiful plants, and will bloom throughout the winter and spring with ordinary attention ; nothing more fully rewarding the care of the cultivator. If any unusually fine flowers should appear, they may be propagated by cuttings in sand under a bell glass ; but it is better to grow the stock every year from seed ; the seed is usually sold mixed, white and pink ; they may be distinguished, almost as soon as they come up, by the color of the stems.

The double varieties, though much sought after, are not, I think, comparable to the single richly fringed ones, and they can only be propagated by cuttings, which is difficult, and uncertain in result, Though both this and the single one are perennials. they require for Green-house culture to be treated as annuals. The other varieties named are treated as perennials, though they may be propagated freely by division of the roots. They are a pretty class of plants, but not very showy or remarkable.

ROSE.

The perpetual varieties are preferred.

Soil—two parts loam, one part rotted manure, one part vegetable fibre and sand.

There are no roses that bloom naturally in the winter or very early spring; indeed, it is indisputably a summer flower; still by skilful management a few blooms may be had, and they are very valuable.

All I can give is a few general hints. Let them be always on their own stocks, not budded; do not force them too rapidly; I have found that the same plants answer three or four years in succession, better than fresh ones. When the plants are turned out of the house, plunge the roses in some open part of the garden, and keep them stopped back throughout the summer, that they may not bloom; take them up in August, repot them and place them in the cold frame; if a successful growth be then started, they will bloom early in the house.

Some cultivators take up plants, of the perpetual varieties, out of the borders, after their first bloom is over, and pot them for winter bloom with success.

SOLLYA.

Heteropylla. Angustifolia.

Soil—Two parts peat, one part loam and sand.

A pretty, half-climbing evergreen, with a blue flower, a free grower and easily managed, but will not do without some support. It must be pruned freely after the bloom is over, and though not naturally a very early bloomer, it will in a year or two accommodate itself to the habit of the house. It must not be put out of doors too early, nor re-potted too freely.

VERONICA.

Andersonii. Speciosa. Odora. Salisifolia.

Soil—Three parts loam, one part vegetable fibre and sand.

A very beautiful plant, not as generally cultivated as it ought to be. The kinds do not all bloom early enough for the winter garden, but a selection may be made, and in a year or two, under the treatment directed, they will bloom earlier.

The first years of rearing them, cut them back freely and early, without regard to the bloom, but not into the old wood, so that they may start their growth before they are put out. Repot but sparingly.

BULBOUS ROOTED PLANTS.

All these have, more or less, a season of rest, when watering or any other exciting course must be withheld, and their activity afterwards is in proportion to the degree of rest. Ample drainage is all important, and the bulb must never be more than half covered with the soil.

AMARYLLIS.

Formosissima. Amabilis. Ignescens. Spectabilis.

Soil—One part peat, one part loam, one part vegetable fibre, and sand enough to secure a porous compost.

This bulb requires absolute rest when the bloom and growth are completed; the shelf in the potting-house is the place for it during that time, when it must be kept entirely without water. In the autumn, winter, or early spring, according to the habits and training of the bulb, it will show signs of activity, when it must be repotted, watered and removed to the Green-house. The growth will now be very rapid and an increasing amount of water will be continually required, until the resting time recurs. It is a very beautiful flower, not difficult to manage, and blooms successfully. Off-shoots, if they appear, should be rubbed off carefully when the bulb goes to rest.

CYCLAMEN.

Persicum Varieties.

Soil—One part peat, one part loam, one part rotted manure, one part sand.

This charming flower is cultivated with very various success. I have seen a window plant with ordinary care flourishing and bearing a hundred blooms, while those in a well ordered Green-house were dwindling and flowerless. It is said that some dealers propagate the plant by dividing the roots, in which case they will always be sickly plants; this may be so, but probably the cause of failure lies in not attending to the alternate periods of activity and rest. About June, although the leaves may not be entirely gone, it will be found the activity of the plant has ceased; it should then be placed in a sheltered situation where it will get no sun or rain, and be kept without water till it shows signs of growth about August or early in September; it must then be repotted, placed in the Green-house, and watered increasingly till it blooms and again rests.

OXALIS.

Tricolor. Bowei. Speciosa.

Soil—Two parts peat, one part loam, one part sand.

Early in September they usually begin to start; divide them, putting three or four tufts in each pot, water them well and put them in a sheltered part of the garden or airy part of the Green-house; in October they should be in active growth, showing bloom. They rest soon after April, when the cold frame or a good shelter will do; water must be gradually withheld.

HYACINTHS, TULIPS, &c.

A few of these, usually called Dutch bulbs, add to the gaiety of the house in spring, and its fragrance also, though, as they require renewing every year, being only fit for the borders afterwards, I sometimes doubt their being worth the cost. A rich, open soil is needed; some of the Harlaem growers use equal parts of rotted manure and sand, and it answers very well. Pot them as soon as you get them, sinking them slightly in the soil, and let them root in a shady place, or buried in sand or ashes, not exposed to rain. Take them into the house, when they are rooted and begin to grow, and water freely.

LILY OF THE VALLEY.

For winter blooming, take matured roots, with well formed buds, in March, and having plunged six inch pots in a shady border, put six or eight in each pot, cover them well and let them grow through the summer, pinching off any blooms that they may throw up. In October they may be treated the same as the Dutch bulbs. The kind of soil is not very important; loam and sand will do.

BEDDING PLANTS.

The green-house should furnish an ample supply of these valuable additions to the borders, and it may be done with comparatively little trouble and even gain to the winter show in the house. Provide in the spring one or two young plants of each kind it is wished to have, put them with the plants in the summer station, and keep the blooming shoots stopped off through the summer. In August pot them into larger pots and allow them to grow on and bloom, which they will then do more or less throughout the winter; when they go into the house with the other plants put them on the upper shelf, as near the glass as may be. You may cut the blooms for bouquets, and in the spring there will be abundance of young shoots for cuttings. Watch against mildew and aphis, and do not over-water them.

Early in March, or as soon as the hot-bed or tan-pit is ready, strike these cuttings in sand under bell-glasses, according to directions given. They will root in about three weeks, and may then be potted in thumb-pots, and after a few days close treatment, put them in the cold frame, plunged in sand or ashes, giving air according to circumstances, but gradually increasing it, that they may be prepared for full exposure early in June. If no bottom-heats be available, the striking may be done in a sheltered corner of the Green-house. In any case, shade the glasses from the sun. I have grown as many as four hundred in one season in this way.

The most useful kinds are:

Verbenas, Scarlet Geraniums, dwarfs preferred, Salvia Fulgens, Patens and Patens Alba. Heliotropes, Ageratum, Gazania.

N. B.—Some of the Salvias rest in winter, and in that case watering must be decreased and finally withheld.

When bedding out, save a plant or two, the strongest of each kind, for similar treatment the next season, pot them at once into large pots, stop them, and proceed as before.

Ordinary soil will do for all these—loam and vegetable fibre with sand. For the plants to be kept through the winter, a little rotted manure may be added.

Heliotropes are so valuable for winter blooms, that two or three additional plants may very well be provided for that purpose, treated in the same way; there are many varieties, some of which are of force more easily than others.

ANNUALS FOR THE GREEN-HOUSE IN SUMMER.

Balsams, especially if the seed be three or four years old, as it should be, require bottom-heat to raise them. New seed does not produce stocky plants, or fine flowers. The soil can hardly be too rich, even if it be half manure, with loam and sand. Pot them as soon as they can be handled; keep them close and warm, with air only in the middle of sunny days, and repot them as soon as the roots begin to mat, which will be surprisingly soon. If they do well, give abundant water, and syringe occasionally overhead, but not in the sunshine. I do not see the necessity for the very numerous shifts some people talk of, but believe it does as well to shift them two or three sizes at once, and then by sinking them as low as possible in the pot, a piece of bare stem is buried, and the laterals brought nearer the rim of the pot. They must on no account be crowded together or they will grow lank stems, and without side branches. Pick off the first blossoms which show themselves on the main stem, and keep them freely growing; by July or August they ought to be in eleven or twelve inch pots, three feet high, two feet across, and with bloom showing at once, on the main stem and side branches. Surely if they are of good quality they are a fine sight. Plenty of water and close treatment in the house will keep them growing and blooming till the Green-house plants come back to their home.

In gathering seed for another year, choose, of course, the plants having the finest and most double flowers, and gather only the smallest pods, even those with only one small seed in them, for those will have come from the most double flowers; for the quality of the flowers varies, not only in different plants grown from the same seed, but also in the same plant.

Martynia Fragrans requires the same treatment with balsam; it is not nearly so eligible a plant, nor have I often seen it grown into a good form; but it makes a little variety in the summer show.

Cockscomb and Amaranthus, make likewise a variety in the summer blooms, but are not particularly interesting. They require a common soil loam and sand, and make fine plants if raised early in a hot-bed.

SPOMEAS—The hot-house varieties require heat to raise them, a good rich soil, and plenty of pot room; it is better to sow them two or three in a pot, and thin out, leaving only one; they do not like transplanting.

ACHIMENES AND GLOXINIA I should not recommend, unless a tan-pit be available. Achimenes are quite dormant in the winter, and may be kept dry on a shelf in the potting-house. As soon as there is a good heat in the pit, turn them out of their pots, and pick out as many of the finest tubers as are required, plant them in seed-pans—pots are unnecessarily deep—in loam and vegetable fibre, with a little sand and rotted manure, two or three inches apart, each way; plunge them in the tan; water slightly at first, increasing it as they grow, and remove them into the Green-house with the summer annuals. They will probably require props, as it is almost impossible to rear them with stems strong enough to carry the blooms. Gloxinias, for the most part, are likewise dormant in the winter, though it is, by many growers, thought better not to dry them off entirely, but any excess of moisture will cause them to decay. They like a very open soil, one-half loam and one-half vegetable fibre, and plenty of sand; repot them when bottom-heat is ready, but do not shake bulbs out of the soil; remove the loose soil only, as far as it can be done without injury to the roots; they like plenty of pot-room; the bulb must be two-thirds above the soil; water sparingly at first, increasing it, as growth proceeds. It is one of the most charming plants grown; it is easily propagated from seed, when new varieties will be obtained, or from striking a leaf in sand; indeed I have struck the flower-stalk, thinking I should perpetuate one of those erect flowers which appear now and then, but the result was a pendant flower like the parent plant, and not like the stray flower I worked upon.

www.ingramcontent.com/pod-product-compliance
Lightning Source LLC
Chambersburg PA
CBHW020322090426
42735CB00009B/1362
* 9 7 8 3 3 3 7 2 5 6 8 6 9 *